811

MW00768485

Stardust otel

A
Richard
Jackson
Book

Also by Paul B. Janeczko

POETRY COLLECTIONS
Strings: A Gathering of Family Poems
Pocket Poems
Poetspeak: In Their Work, About Their Work
Dont Forget to Fly
Postcard Poems
Going Over to Your Place
This Delicious Day: 65 Poems
The Music of What Happens
The Place My Words Are Looking For
Preposterous: Poems of Youth
Looking for Your Name

ORIGINAL POETRY
Brickyard Summer

FICTION
Bridges to Cross

NONFICTION
Loads of Codes and Secret Ciphers

In
Memoriam

*Christine
Edris*

Orchard Books
New York

Poems by
PAUL B. JANECZKO

Illustrations by
Dorothy Leech

Stardust otel

ORCHARD BOOKS
95 Madison Avenue
New York, NY 10016

LIBRARY OF CONGRESS CATALOGING-IN-PUBLICATION DATA
Janeczko, Paul B.
Stardust otel : poems / by Paul B. Janeczko;
illustrations by Dorothy Leech.
p.   cm.
"A Richard Jackson Book."
Summary: A series of poems in which a young boy describes his
life with his flower children parents, his friends, and neighbors.
ISBN 0-531-05498-5. -- ISBN 0-531-08648-8 (lib. bdg.)
1. Young adult poetry, American. [1. American poetry.]
I. Leech, Dorothy, ill.   II. Title.
PS3560.A465S7 1993
811'.54--dc20   92-44514

Manufactured in the United States of America
Book design by Dorothy Leech

10 9 8 7 6 5 4 3 2 1

The text of this book is set in Lubalin Graph, Korinna, and Nofret.
The illustrations are ink wash on scratchboard.

*For Emma
Kathryn
Janeczko*

> *Oh, how you
> have touched
> my mad,
> astonished
> heart*

Contents

History:
Stardust   otel

M y parents—
flower children,
Woodstock lovers—
named me Leary
after their hero

insisted I call them Nick and Lucy

bought a house:
three floors,
tired brown clapboards,
a long front porch
hanging like a pouting lower lip

named it
after powdering their faces with stardust
in a psychedelic vision.

T he H fell nearly 15 years ago:
the day I was born
Nick swung on it in joy
until it snapped off in his hands.
He never replaced it,
saying he liked to be reminded
of how he felt that day.

Treasures

NICK:

San Francisco Giants cap
with a spot,
dirty from tugging,
on the visor

Hickory-handled framing hammer
his father used
to build the house Nick was born in

One of my baby shoes,
never bronzed,
dusty and soft

Bail receipts
from protest-march arrests
stuffed into a Nixon hand puppet

Letters
from Nick
stuck with stamps of generals and bright birds,
bound by a dark green ribbon

A silver watch
with numbers nearly too small to read,
a gift from her father to her mother
before he went to war

The Team

W hen everybody showed—
those games that didn't conflict
with clarinet lessons,
visits from aunts smelling of rose water,
and altar-boy practice—
there were nine of us.

Tony didn't stray far from first,
never smiled,
scolded his glove, The Claw,
when he muffed one.

Patrick played second,
chattered
No-batter-no-batter,
spit into the pocket of his glove.

Pacing at short,
Randy always seemed to be
headed in the right direction
to snag the ball
and inspect it
before rifling it to first.

T homas claimed the hot corner
but no one complained,
happy to avoid
the broken nose
concussion
split lip
that had found him.

14

Wayne roamed in left,
called Time!
whenever he chased down a ball
so he could comb his hair
and adjust his cap
with precision
for the girls who strolled
on the other side of the line.

Before every batter
I checked on John,
big-boned daydreamer in center
whose smile made me feel
I was missing something.

*M*ost of us didn't like Arthur,
who played right,
but we loved
the way he gunned the ball
to any place on the field.

Brady on the mound
chewed Juicy Fruit,
toed the rubber,
bragged he could throw a curve,

and me crouched behind the plate
watching through bars
ready to block his blunders.

15

Becky

B ecky Loudermilk
had brown eyes, sad
even when she laughed,
bony angles,
taller than most boys in our class,
"Loudermouth" to some,
liked: talking to herself,
Milk Duds,
and forgery,
charging one dollar
for a signature
on a report card or test paper,
two to write a note.
Charged me half.
Friend.

Everybody knew
her father drank,
  shouted,
    argued,
      once picked a fight with an oak.
So no one said a word
when she visited at suppertime
(Lucy believed in cooking enough
for unexpected guests),
or even stayed the night
in the small corner room
with flowery pink wallpaper.
No one said a word.
Friends.

Casualties

C harlie Hooper didn't say much
except when he sat on the porch swing
at night,
and talked of
baseball
cars
girls he almost married,
a voice
behind the orange dot of his cigarette,
the darkness
hiding his restless eyes,
his steel-pinned leg
that dragged behind him
like an afterthought,
that pained him in stormy weather.

H e was waiting,
he told me,
in a voice that was quiet but wild
like pigeons taking flight,
for his army buddies—
Tub, Ernie, and Satch—
so the four could cruise
to Florida in his van
for hot sun and (he grinned) women to match.

He even showed me their picture
in fatigues and helmets
outside a hooch in An Loc,
saying,

> All crazier'n hell
> Tub smoked these black cigars
> that smelled like burning hair
> Satch liked to sketch
> animals on scraps of paper
> Once Ernie picked up
> the back end of a jeep
> with a general parked in it
> We never visited Saigon bars
> without Ernie.

I believed him
until by chance I saw
the brittle clipping that told
how three soldiers died
—one escaped unharmed—
when a bomb exploded in a Saigon bar.

So I stayed away from the porch,
telling myself I had other things to do
when the creak of the swing
reminded me of my fear,
until a rainy Saturday
when he tossed his duffel bag in the van
and drove away
taking what I had added
to his harm.

Thomas

Never Tom.
Tommy got you a headlock
until you gave him
what he wanted: Thomas,
as in Edison, Jefferson, or
Gould, his uncle,
who impersonated Elvis
in Gulf-Coast bars.

Worked at his ambitions:

R ed Sox TV announcer:
turned off the sound,
supplied his own play-by-play,
interviewed teammates
after a victory

T op-40 disc jockey:
listened to records,
talked smooth fast sentences
without periods

S tuntman:
walked with a war limp in church,
grabbed his gut
and crashed into trash cans,
slid his bike to the ground
and rolled through clouds of dust

and
Playboy photographer
(or at least the one who
carried lemonade to the models):
studied the magazine
and dreamed of lemons.

21

The Natural

Some adults called Jackie Slattery
hot-rodder,
wise guy,
punk,
but he only smirked and said,
"At least they notice me,"
just the way we saw girls notice
him in overalls,
grease streaked across the front.

Jackie worked at the Sun station
where Mr. Jasper, the owner,
usually tipped back in a chair
against the Pepsi machine,
said Jackie was a natural with cars,
and we figured like he was
a natural with the girls
who visited him at the station
after Mr. Jasper had gone home
and Jackie worked on his Ford.
Girls we never saw around school.
Girls in spiked heels,
leopard pants snug
as a stamp on a first-class parcel, and
lips painted
any color but red.
Girls whose laughter danced
to us on the bench at the curb
imagining.

*U*ntil the May night
he left with a girl
and never came back.
What came back was a rumor—
Jackie married
with a family on the way—
which we refused to believe,
picturing instead
Jackie's Ford in flames
at the finish line
as he beats another stranger
on a blacktop straightaway.

Nesterenko

We knew
Pearl was sick, but
not how sick
until Nesterenko canceled
the lessons he gave on the parlor piano,
skipped supper, and
stayed up all night crooning
softly to the small poodle
until the end came.

Because Nesterenko asked,
I carried Pearl,
light as an empty hornets' nest,
to the hole he had dug.

There was no music from him
for three weeks;
we wondered
if it was buried with Pearl.
Until a Sunday after lunch
when he visited Pearl,
approached the piano
like a stranger on a dance floor,
and sat down,
looked at his fingers,
at the keys the color of his tobacco-stained teeth,
and began,
slowly, slowly at first,
like the beginning of a spring rain,
until the notes flooded
the house with their storm.

24

Names

Edward Giantonio—
thin as a hacksaw blade,
with a mustache
that looked penciled in—
changed his name,
calling himself

Eduardo
on Thursdays
when he gave samba lessons
to ladies in a rented room
over Owen's Auto Parts

Eddie the Stick
Fast Eddie
other nights
when he circled a green felt table
at the Eight Ball

Ed
when he washed dishes
at Duke's Diner

and Eddie G
when he hung out
at the Boxcar
telling stories
of fast women in faraway cities

*U*ntil Anita Willoughby
the night waitress
stopped working
because of the twins in her.
Then he called himself
gone,
leaving
a pair of narrow black slacks
on a metal hanger.

Drive-in

The Hilltop Drive-in lasted
until the new mall reminded people
that there was no need
for the distraction of stars
when they watched a movie,
and the Buxton brothers strung a rusty chain
across the entrance,
tacked a Keep Out sign on an elm.

*I*gnoring the sign,
we leaped the chain,
Becky's braid flapping,
and sat on a bench
in front of the boarded snack bar,
watching the clouds
coast across the crescent moon
above the torn movie screen

silent

until
our bare arms touched,
sparking her hand
to take mine,
making the words I had planned to say
vanish
like a cloud of bats
into the night.

Fixer

Nick liked to fix things:
a radio that wouldn't stop playing
unless you pulled the plug,
a door that took two to open
when we had rain,
a blender that smoked,
a washer that growled.

Lucy called him Gadget King,
flushed when she thought of our cellar
with its paths, like rabbit runs, past
coils of wire,
coffee cans full of screws, nuts, and bolts,
TV tubes hanging like hams in a smokehouse,
how-to books and repair manuals
stacked in the corner.
When she complained about the mess,
threatened
"to put a match to the whole damn place,"
he snorted, "She always says that.
Till she needs something down there."

When doctors discovered cancer
raging in Grandpa,
Nick spent his days and nights
with his father,
anger working on him
like a dull saw on oak.

*G*randpa died
in the middle of the night.
Nick returned
to sit on the back steps
alone until
I, knowing in my sleep,
found him, puffy eyed.
He pulled me to him.
"Life's easier," he said,
"if you know
what can be fixed
and what can't."

And that was all
as we sat
watching
the day's pink start.

Wanda

Being told to steer clear,
the closest I ever came
to the Boxcar Lounge
was the bus-stop bench at the curb,
the one gouged with initials and awkward hearts.
That's where we sat
waiting for Wanda,
the black woman who sang
with a piano player at the Boxcar.
When I told Thomas
she reminded me of a serpent
in her green grass,
he reminded me of what a serpent did to Adam.
Men, leaning against cars,
smoking cigarettes,
stared at her dress and nodded
through smiles to her,
but she winked at me.

I never heard her sing at the Boxcar,
smoky and filled with watchers,
but late at night
when she walked slowly up the stairs
singing softly,
I knew it was just for me.

Elixir

When he couldn't get a date
for the Snowflake Ball
in the decorated gym

because Sally Kirby, cheerleader,
who was loved by thin sweaters and
boys just out of reform school,
laughed in his face,

because Jean Fox, library aide,
who never spoke above a whisper,
said she'd let him know
then didn't,

Wayne begged me to go with him
to visit Madame Belinsky,
Herbalist of Kings and Queens,
in her parlor between the A&P and the pet shop,
which was dark
and smelled of roses.

Eyes shut, she sat in a shiny black robe,
silver hair shooting from her head
like lightning.
Even as I whispered, "She looks dead,"
her eyelids were rising.
"Come,"
she said slowly,
the single word a flame
drawing moths.
She laid a hand on Wayne's.
"I feel problems with women."

Wayne shrugged.
"You need the elixir
to repair your damaged aura."
"The what?"
"Hair of an ox from Mesopotamia,
powdered fin of the hammerhead shark,
dung of the white Tibetan crow
mixed in the shadow of Vesuvius,
aged in the temple of Moc-Moc,
Malaysian god of fertility."

W ayne handed over six dollars
and we left
with a small brown bottle
and directions
to sprinkle it on his body
on the night of the next full moon.

As we walked home
Wayne said he didn't know if
he could wait
to sprinkle himself with the magic.

Then Annie Preston, new to school,
winked and smiled at him
from a table in the sandwich shop.

As Wayne pushed open the door
he tossed me his magic
not even bothering to ask
how he looked.

Hands

Maisie Whitman was known
around town as "that pretty lady
barber."
I'd go for my haircut
when I knew Pinky's was crowded,
giving me a chance
to sit and watch her
over the top of *Field and Stream*
though I always lost my nerve
and slid into Pinky's chair.
I needed to sit
when I looked at her face:
eyes that startled
with their green,
blond hair falling
across her forehead
over one eye.

She'd cut until five,
hurry to her room, dragging
the smell of Old Spice and talc through the hallway,
grab something from the refrigerator—
a cold pork chop or a couple of carrots—
before she rushed out back
to the sagging garage
to work on the '57 Chevy Impala
—dented where it wasn't rusted—
a car she'd won
in a poker game in Pinky's back room.

O ne night when she saw me
leaning against the door, watching her work,
she smiled and asked me
to hand her a crescent wrench.
I wound up being, as she said,
her extra hands,
listening to exotic talk
of carburation, valves, and torque
until it got too dark to work
and we retreated to the corner sink,
scooped Lava,
worked up a lather
until she snatched my hands
and lathered some more
as our laughter bubbled into the night.

Prince of the
Dump

Saturdays late
Owen Forbes,
Prince of the Dump,
and his one-eyed dog, Wink,
chased those
who'd stopped to swap news and lies.

C igar butt
smoldering in a Woolworth corncob pipe
to keep the bugs at bay,
gnarled walking stick,
sharp eye of a spy,
which some said he was
(though we never asked)
before he moved into the small house
on the Dump Road,
added one room, another
since Owen's passion was salvage,
from Wink,
left to die in a trash bag,
to

trophies
Rec League Softball Camps 1985
4-H First Prize Sow
Perfect Attendance Baptist Sunday School
among his favorites;

books
inscribed by unknown people
to those they loved;

photos
mostly black-and-white
stacked in a beer case,
except the one
he slid into a silver frame:
smiling mother, father, sweet-faced girl
forever happy.

Evil Eye

"Seeing the future is not difficult,"
Mrs. Cassalli told us
as we sat in a room that smelled
of garlic and strong red wine,
"if you can read the evil eye."

We looked at the rose-colored mixing bowl
sitting on the coffee table.
"You pour olive oil on water
and read its shape. Or,"
with a wink she added,
"holy water makes more magic."
Then, with a squint she whispered,
"But the best way
is the way I choose:
to mix holy water from different churches."

As she tipped the oil cruet
we leaned forward
to see the oil sink in a stream
before it blobbed back to the surface.

With dark sad eyes
she peered into the bowl,
breaking the silence to tell us,
"One of you will go to college.
One of you will marry young
but happily.
One of you will travel far.
One of you will make a great discovery.
And one of you
will be lost."

38

"Which is which?" Wayne asked.
Eyes closed, she shook her head.
"For that,
you must come back
one at a time."

We joked on the way to the field,
making fun of a fortune-teller
who couldn't read
tea leaves or your palm.

But, afraid to find out
we'd been wrong,
none of us ever went back.

Mail-Order Romance

A lthough she worked
at Four Winds Travel,
Alice Singer never traveled
except to the front porch
to collect her latest shipment
of mail-order romance novels.

A jolly person,
freely dispensing travel trivia
in the form of a question—
as in, Did you know
the summertime temperature in Hong Kong
averages 87 degrees?—
she became nervous and abrupt
the day her new books were delayed
between Hollywood and her hands,
and she neared the last page
of her last book.
She cornered me in the kitchen,
begged me to follow her
to her room,
which startled me
with its disarray.
"I was searching for one book
I might have overlooked,"
she mumbled.
She crossed to a pile of paperbacks
and reached into it,
as if she were going to pull
the winning ticket for a Christmas turkey,
and snatched a broken-spined book
and thrust it at me.

"Read," she begged.
"Maybe it will sound different
with a man reading it."

She slumped into her chair,
closed her eyes,
and whispered, "Read."
I swallowed.

S ix pages after I began
reading *Ecstasy at Falconwood Mansion*
at the spot where the book had flopped open,
she began to tremble,
to moan,
to call the hero's name.

B efore she could open her eyes
and see
it was only me,
I was saved
from her heaving bosom
and pudgy alabaster arms
by the thud of a package
hitting the front porch.

First Snow

*W*e sat in the bleachers
behind first base,
watching the field deepen with snow,
talking of things white:
clouds, swans, meringue,
until Becky powdered her lips with snow;
I shivered
feeling the kiss
of icy strawberries.

*T*hen she was gone,
running past the place where
first base was buried,
digging crookedly for second
as she looked over her shoulder,
saw me in hot pursuit.
She shrieked,
scooped snow,
and flung it in my direction.
I would have caught her at third
but for an unintentional slide
that carried me into foul territory
as she raced toward home.
Crawling,
slipping,
I followed,
gaining on her
until we slid home together,
safe in our laughter.

Rusty

Rusty Hughes played
his entire career at Louisville
except for three games
with the Cardinals at the end of '78
when they battled the Mets
to avoid the cellar.

Now
he helps with the high school team:
hitting grounders,
barking praise,
and talking about the Show;

enjoys unfolding
a tattered sports-page box score,
pointing to his name,
and, with a smile,
the 1 in the H column;

but mostly
works at the A&P,
fielding questions
about chicken thighs,
Cornish hens,
and leg of lamb;

fiddles with the radio dial
with the nervous hands of a shortstop,
searching the static
for faraway games
and the sound of his name.

Bully

P hilip Slade, 17-year-old ninth grader,
picked specks of tobacco
from the tip of his tongue,
showed off teeth
the color of wet cement,
and looked for kids to bully
the way a Boy Scout looked for
old ladies perched on curbs:

mocking Marci Carlton's stutter
until she fled the cafeteria in tears
trailed by friends,

hanging a dead crow in Todd Lambert's locker
the day after his father's funeral,

saying he wanted to "talk" to you after school,
knowing you'd hide in the janitor's room
and take the long way home in the dark.

U ntil a curve ended
the joyride,
his mother's car
rolling
over
over
after throwing him
into its haphazard path.

No one in our class visited him
in his wheelchair,
not caring to take
the long way
home.

45

Photos

We didn't have a family album.
No gold-lettered brown leather cover
over plastic pages for us.
We had a shoe box.
Nick's size-11 Adidas Super Trainer box,
rubber banded to keep the lid in line.

W hen the time was right,
Nick carried the Family Shoe Box
to the kitchen table,
poured half a glass of
his homemade wine,
as dark as an eggplant's hide,
and slid back the lid.

He didn't say much
as we thumbed through a tangle of the past:

Jimi Hendrix
prancing onstage
        "Woodstock"

Grandpa
red faced
carving a bulging turkey
        "Pop's last Christmas"

Lucy
wearing cap and softball jersey
for Friendly Ford
        "The *real* Babe"

Dennis Swan
Nick's college roommate
smiling in his army uniform
        "Never came back"

Nick
grinning, holding
me, howling in a blue blanket
        "Three days old"

W hen Lucy suggested order,
Nick, gathering the pictures, scoffed,
"You don't want memories in order.
Half the fun is the surprise,
not knowing what comes next."

47

*D*ancer

Ernest Hyde worked at Moyer's Memorial Chapel,
helping ready the bodies,
every now and then
driving the hearse.

He looked the part
with solemn face
dark blue suit
and shiny shoes.
Wavy hair.
White carnation in his lapel.

Simile

B ut every Saturday night
he swapped his suit for
a sports shirt—
he was partial to paisley—
and pleated pants
and visited
the singles-only dance at the Y
where his feet glided
like water spiders
or blurred
like a prizefighter's,
depending on his partner
and the tune.

48

*H*e danced
with all the ladies
who weren't spooked
by being held by someone
who touched the dead,
sometimes one on each arm,
with a smile wide enough
for all the living.
He even danced with the waitress—
a plump woman named Lydia
with hair the color of steel wool,
thick ankles,
and lopsided white shoes—
before he drove her home in the hearse
and talked of gardens,
music,
and the moonlit night.

One and Only

When Millie Benson called me "Sunshine,"
I knew something was up.

Three husbands—
twice divorced,
used a private eye
to track down Number Three
to retrieve her Camaro and ceramic Elvis head—
she was sour on Saturdays
when she came to wash the bedding,
dust the rooms,
and organize the linen closet,
grumbling like a cranky dog
about low-down men, and
how the world would be
better without them, and
too bad I was going
to grow up
to be one.

"Sunshine," she sang,
"I finally found the right man.
Don't know how I kept it
secret so long.
Lights my cigarettes,
dances like a dream,
calls me his one and only."

I was happy for her
until she told me
the man was Buzz Pinckney,
whom I'd spied walking
along the tracks two days before,
arm around the thin waist of a woman
in a dress the color of butter.

"I can feel it," Millie said.
"*This* time it's going to be different."

She set off down the stairs,
whistling,
but I still heard Buzz calling
the thin woman
his one and only.

Mr. Loudermilk

*T*hey weren't sure
who pulled the trigger:
Becky, tired of being beaten;
her mother, hungry for calm;
or the dead man himself,
careless with drink.

To me, it never mattered,
I had wanted him dead
so many times:
when Becky tried to hide a new bruise,
or said, "He didn't mean it."

*W*hat mattered was that Becky left
for good
after the funeral
as quietly as a cat
slipping into tall grass
before I could tell her
that she reminded me of the wild roses
growing madly over a sunny stone wall
by the railroad tracks.

Then I wished the man alive,
missing Becky
as I did.

Dare

The dare bloomed
out of our nothing-to-do chatter
like a lily from a compost heap:
"Bet you can't do it."
"You'll see," I said.

Then came talk with purpose—
setting the time (that very night)
for the deed:
kissing the gravestone
of Hannah Parker,
twenty years dead at the age of sixteen.

We met at the edge
of the burying ground,
restless in the rain
that made the gravestones shine.
Wayne announced,
"She's at the end of this row,"
but we all knew
where the smooth snowy angel marked
her grave
as surely as no one knew
how Hannah had died or
who had paid for the angel.
There was always talk,
but the truth lay buried with her.

"Y ou really going to do it?" John asked.
I told him it was just a slab of stone
before I turned, eyes on the angel,
and walked past the dead toward Hannah.
I grinned back at my friends,
huddled, holding their breath,
turned to see Hannah had a face:
a photo,
an oval set in the stone,
caught her straight yellow hair,
grin,
and eyes that looked surprised to see
me.

"Do it!" Arthur yelled,
the others quiet
(seeing me start to shake?)
as I slowly bent
and pressed my dry lips
to the polished marble.

M y shakes grew into a trot,
a run that carried me
past the grins and praise of friends,
as I had gone beyond our bargain:
to kiss the cold face of death.

Radio
Weather Lady

We fell in love with her
voice.

F irst, Wayne
when he heard Maggie Beal
give the weather on the local radio station
(WONE, The *Big* One!)
one day after school
and immediately began writing a love letter
and researching marriage laws in the state.
Then Thomas, doubting at first,
only had to hear her
dish out the weekend forecast and
he was easily converted,
believing she was a model,
skin as smooth as a wet bar of Ivory,
waiting for her Big Break.
Finally me
as we listened one Friday.
They'd been right:
it was the way she said
"stormy weather" and
"cumulus clouds,"
cooing,
caressing each word
the way we imagined
she'd say our names.

*U*ntil we visited the station
and had Maggie Beal pointed out to us
as she was leaving
in her plainness
and dull brown hair,
climbing into a battered red pickup
with two kids waiting,
with John Beal, Plumber
painted on the doors.

*T*homas felt cheated.
"It's not fair" was how he put it.
Wayne denied
he ever really cared about her.
They said they'd never listen
to Maggie Beal again.
I agreed and didn't
except now and then
late at night
when I hushed my breathing
and listened to her words:
plush,
silky,
roses nodding in the fog.

For Sale

L ucy's other passions—
gardening, writing letters, drawing—
kept her at home.
But on the first Saturday of each month
she cleared the table
and spread the classifieds
before her like a map.
Marker in hand,
she scanned the columns,
circling each estate sale,
then planning her itinerary to save
jewelry heirs didn't care about.

S ome days she returned early,
empty-handed,
the good pieces selling fast.
But on other days
she returned eager to share
her prizes with us:
pins and brooches,
now and then a cameo
or a locket
with a tiny photo of a smiling stranger
whose life Lucy had saved.

59

So Many Days

I never thought about it
until Todd Lambert's father—
younger than Nick,
thinner, tan—dropped
dead
while mowing the lawn.

No warning, Todd said.
Never sick.
Just fell to his knees
then over on his side
as if sleeping
with broken glasses.

Which made me shadow Nick,
looking for strain and exertion,
and do chores with new enthusiasm:
hauling trash, raking leaves, and,
most important, mowing the lawn.
Until Nick grew suspicious
and cornered me over a glass of lemonade.
"It's not Father's Day," he began,
making a face
as if he had a real puzzle on his hands,
"and my birthday's not for months."

60

After my explanation
he said, "We get so many days. Period.
Not one more, not one less
than we're entitled to."

ick squeezed my shoulder.
"I appreciate your help,"
he said, "I do,
but worry doesn't make life
smoother."
He drained his glass,
looked at it with regret,
and set it on the table
before walking outside,
ready to tempt fate
with the pull of the lawn-mower cord.

Ghosts

When we talked of being ghosts

I went for the comic:
wanting to
lift Mr. Steinberg's black toupee
and toss it,
tangle it in his forsythias,
ride a bike down the center of the street,
and maybe open the automatic door at the A&P.

*T*homas wanted to haunt:
Marty Willard,
who pushed his face into dirty snow
after the fifth-grade Christmas pageant;
Mrs. Magruder,
who mocked his tales
explaining homework undone;
his father,
who left two days before
Thomas turned ten
without saying why.

*W*ayne didn't care to be a ghost,
just invisible
so he could visit places
he ached to see:
the girls' locker room
after a varsity basketball game,
the backseats of cars
parked overlooking the river,
and Sally Kirby's bedroom
in moonlight
when her pillow flamed
with her red hair.

Mrs. Talbot

Mrs. Talbot seldom spoke
or left her room.

Lucy said
it was because her heart, broken
with the passing
of family and friends,
would not let her forget.

Others thought her crazy:
chasing church ladies
who brought casseroles and salvation,
singing mournful hymns
while she watched game shows,
rocking on the porch in the dark,
the creak a second heartbeat.

I wasn't sure
until my dream:
I open her door.
Mrs. Talbot, a sleek songbird
with red and orange feathers,
rushes onto the porch,
bursts into flight,
soaring
as her song grows louder,
circling
as her wings grow stronger,
until she vanishes,
and I walk away
humming her farewell hymn.

63

811